Profiles In Fashion
Vera Wang

J B WANG, V. PET
Petrillo, Lisa
Vera Wang

Profiles In Fashion
Vera Wang

By Lisa Petrillo

MORGAN
REYNOLDS
P U B L I S H I N G

Greensboro, North Carolina

Profiles in Fashion

Jimmy Choo

Marc Jacobs

Isaac Mizrahi

Kate Spade

Vera Wang

Profiles in Fashion: Vera Wang

Library of Congress Cataloging-in-Publication Data

Petrillo, Lisa.
  Vera Wang / by Lisa Petrillo. -- 1st ed.
      p. cm. -- (Profiles in fashion)
  Includes bibliographical references and index.
  ISBN 978-1-59935-150-6
  1. Wang, Vera--Juvenile literature. 2. Women fashion designers--United
States--Biography--Juvenile literature. 3. Fashion designers--United
States--Biography--Juvenile literature. 4. Fashion designers--New York
(State)--New York--Biography--Juvenile literature. 5. Wedding
costume--United States--Juvenile literature. I. Title.
  TT505.W36P48 2011
  746.9'2092--dc22
  [B]
                                    2010017978

Printed in the United States of America
First Edition

Designed by:
Ed Morgan, navyblue design studio
Greensboro, NC

To Carmela and Lex,
for all the beauty they have brought to life

Contents

1

Inspiration

When Vera Wang was eight years old her father gave her ice skates for Christmas. C. C. Wang had learned to skate as a boy on the lakes of his native China. He took his daughter to Central Park's sailboat pond, which had frozen over that day, to skate, and Vera never forgot the experience: "I fell in love with it—the speed, the flow, and the wind in my face."

C. C. Wang probably didn't realize that Christmas that his daughter would spend a great deal of the first part of her life on skates.

Vera was born into a family of wealth and privilege on June 27, 1949, in New York City. Her brother Kenneth was born two years later. Both C. C. Wang and his wife, Florence, were born in China. C. C., which stands for Cheng Ching, came to the United States in 1943 to obtain a master's degree in chemical engineering from the Massachusetts Institute of Technology (MIT). Then, with three classmates from MIT, he founded an international pharmaceutical distribution company, a trading company, and an oil refining business.

Vera grew up in the most exclusive parts of New York City and Paris—with servants, the most fashionable clothes, and exposure to the world's best restaurants, theaters, and museums.

Florence Wang inspired Vera by exposing her to the world's greatest artwork and fashion. The family's luxurious apartment was filled with museum-quality furnishings. On their walls hung masterpieces from the great Impressionist painters Pierre-Auguste Renoir and Claude Monet.

It was routine for the family to travel to Europe for the art, the culture, and the annual fashion shows introducing the latest in fashion. "I had a mother who was superbly chic," Wang said. "She made fashion this adventure for me as a young woman. She viewed fashion not as superficial but as expressive. That's a big difference."

Her father also loved beautiful things, and as a scientist and successful international businessman he paid close attention to exacting details. His suits were custom-made in Europe, his eyeglasses kept in fancy Hermes cases. "I had an immense education from them in everything, not only fashion but in art and painting," said Wang. "They were very sophisticated people, and yet they loved Dunkin' Donuts too."

C. C. and Florence encouraged Vera and her brother to embrace both their American and Chinese culture with great energy. Vera learned Mandarin as well as French and other languages, and her parents made sure she appreciated Chinese cuisine and traditions as well.

Waterlilies, by Claude Monet, on exhibit at MoMA,
the Museum of Modern Art in New York City.

Strong Roots in an Ancient Land

Vera Wang's family can trace its roots in China back several generations. Her mother grew up in palaces. Florence was the youngest daughter of Wu Yue Shin and Wu Jing Biao, a general who served as the military governor of their province. She was born at the height of World War I in 1918, and in those days, women were expected to honor and serve men, as well as subjugate themselves. In the early twentieth century girls were not encouraged to seek higher education, in China and even in the United States. But Vera's mother defied tradition. Florence finished her schooling and went on to earn a college degree. She came to America in the 1940s to work as a translator for the United Nations.

Vera's father also hailed from China's elite class. He was the younger son of Wang Han Su and Wang Wen Shuen, a general who became a war minister for the legendary ruler Chaing Kai-shek. Chaing Kai-shek was the political and military leader of the Kuomintang of China, or the Chinese National Party—a political party of the Republic of China (Taiwan).

In China C. C. earned a chemistry degree and worked at an oil refinery for more than two years, during which time he learned the oil business, where he would later make his fortune. He served in the Chinese Nationalist army from 1941 to 1943, rising to the rank of lieutenant colonel. While serving in the military, he married Florence.

In 1943, as World War II raged, the couple lived apart when he went to America to earn his master's degree in chemical engineering from the Massachusetts Institute of Technology. When she joined him in New York he had already founded his first company and the couple settled in the Upper East Side of New York City. But deep ties to their homeland remained.

C. C. prospered. Like many of his fellow business tycoons, he loved and supported the arts. But his main passion was golf, and he owned his own course. He also owned homes in Manhattan, rural New York, the beach resort of Southampton, Palm Beach, Florida, as well as in Singapore and Shanghai.

Vera's mother died in 2004, and her father in 2006. To Vera, her parents represented the successful combination of the traditions of ancient China and the energy of young America. "They were both rebellious in their own way. To follow my father to America was unheard of. We're not talking Gloria Steinem (the feminist leader). We're talking almost bound feet. She was a courageous, artistic, passionate woman, and she continued to parade that light into what worlds were possible for me."

European fashion and culture were great influences on Vera,
as her family often traveled to cities like Paris.

The Wangs sent Vera to one of the most elite private schools in Manhattan, the Chapin School. An all-girl, private day school, Chapin was founded at the turn of the twentieth century by Maria Bowen Chapin, a progressive educator and suffragette. Chapin School's motto is *Fortiter et Recte* (Bravely and Rightly), a demonstration of the founder's determination to get women to speak up for what is right.

Above all else, the Wangs believed in working hard. It wasn't enough for Vera to excel in a demanding school. She also studied piano, ballet, and took tennis lessons. But skating was her passion. She started taking lessons at the Skating Club of New York. Soon she was competing, traveling to other states, going to lessons at all hours of the day and night, and squeezing in training between her demanding school schedule.

Vera wanted her skating flow to be graceful, like the wind. She kept up her ballet training as well by studying at one of the finest and most elite ballet schools in the country, the American Ballet School, under the legendary dancer George Balanchine, who was known as an exacting perfectionist. Balanchine's school was located in the Lincoln Center, the home of Manhattan's opera house.

No matter how busy their lives were, Florence made time to take her children to Europe. This early exposure ensured that their love of the arts remained strong throughout their life.

When Vera traveled to Paris with her mother she experienced the seasonal unveiling of new fashions, with shows by top designers like Christian Dior and Hubert de Givenchy. These glamorous affairs attracted the most stylish and wealthy women of the world.

While in Europe, her mother would take her on side trips to places such as Versailles, the palace where Marie Antoinette and King Louis XIV lived in the eighteenth century. It was exciting to Vera to realize her own mother had lived in palaces in China, too.

Florence would have private viewings at the most stylish fashion houses, such as that of Yves St. Laurent. This allowed

Orangery at Château de Versailles in France

Vera to meet the fashion designers and to watch and learn. The memories and designs meant so much to Vera that she saved many of her mother's dresses, preserving them like works of art.

When the Wangs traveled abroad, they didn't jet over the Atlantic Ocean, even though international air travel was becoming more frequent. They traveled aboard luxury ocean liners like the Queen Mary. Ocean liners provided a more leisurely and refined way to travel. Passengers dressed for fancy dinners and socialized along the way with others from the elite class. Wang recalls, "What a fantasyland—I had free run of the ship. Back then, travel wasn't about speed, it was about the process."

2

Vera Takes Off

hen she competed in ice skating Vera had nerves of steel, rarely crumpling from the pressure. At the same time her delicate frame and natural grace helped her give the appearance of floating across the ice. By the age of ten, she was winning medals and championships and traveled the United States to compete. As the *New York Times* once reported, "She performed flawlessly," and the paper called her "exceedingly graceful."

Training meant rising before dawn and skating for hours before school. She would then head to a full school day, then rush through homework, and return to the rink for more training. Every day she spent struggling to land harder jumps, trying to jump higher and higher, and to make her spins faster and longer lasting. She focused on making her school figures (figure eights) flawless, and she practiced her competition free skate routines so they would be so perfect, with all the jumps landing cleanly and the artistic expression soulful.

It was a high-pressure life. Once, on the way to a competition, the car broke down and they were stranded for hours.

She made it to the rink with only ten minutes to prepare, and she went out on the ice and skated her best, not letting the stressful situation ruffle her. She won the competition, showing her grace under pressure.

One of her coaches was Sonya Dunfield, who admired her pupil's self discipline, rare in someone so young. "She was very willing to work hard. She had a passion and a hunger for skating."

Figure skating is a special combination of sport and art. It is the rare sport where competitors must look calm and even smile, never letting the judges and the audience see them sweat. Skaters train hard for years but in the end they only get a brief moment, less than four minutes of performance, to win the glory of the titles and the medals. Wang's friend, Michelle Kwan, another Chinese American skater, who would achieve fame as a champion in the 1990s, described the sport this way:

> At the end of a day . . . your body aches everywhere. Your back hurts from doing layback spins. Your bottom hurts from falling. Your shoulders, your legs—you just hurt all over. But there's still more to do. You work all year on your program until you can do it in your sleep. You practice each jump thousands of times. And then it all comes down to four minutes on the ice! Your skating life can forever be changed by what happens during those four minutes.

Vera's fashionable mother Florence got involved in the creation of her daughter's ice skating outfits. All outfits had to be custom-made, for practice as well as competitions. There were no such things as ready-made outfits you could buy at the store. The stretchy fabrics of today like Spandex were still decades away from being invented. Skaters needed proper clothes to keep up their appearance, but also serviceable outfits able to handle hard wear, the constant falling, banging, snagging on

Michelle Kwan from the U.S. spins during her short program at the World Figure Skating Championships in Lausanne, Switzerland, in March 1997.

sharp blades, heavy washing to get the sweat out, the stretching of a lifetime, but still hold its shape.

The Wangs agreed that Vera's outfits should have great style and not just look like exercise clothes. She must be dressed to be noticed but never cross the line into gaudy. Even as a child, Vera was savvy enough to realize that a skater's appearance mattered. Skating is a sport that judges score—so much of it is left to judges' opinion more than fact. So impressing judges is of utmost importance. Even off the ice at events and competitions where judges would be, many smart skaters like Vera knew they should look their best. Some of her fellow skaters didn't have the maturity or awareness of how important image could be, but young Vera was aware of the whole package. "I was always involved in all aspects of skating, not just the technique, the choreography, the music, but the visual aspects, too —how I looked, what I should wear," Vera said.

As she advanced in skating, Vera sought a coach who could help her reach the top ranks. She found a pro she considered one of the greatest trainers in the world, Pierre Brunet. The European-born Brunet had won world championships as a

Outfits should not only be fashionable but have flexibility to do extreme jumps. Vera understood the complications of this early on. Sasha Cohen competing in the women's short program at the Winter Olympics in Salt Lake City, 2002

singles skater and a pairs skater, and he had trained Olympic medal winners, which is what Vera wanted to be.

In the skating world, Brunet was known for pushing the boundaries of the sport. He and his partner introduced daring athleticism and more interesting fashions. In the old days the women pair skaters—those who skated in tandem with men—wore white dresses until Brunet's female partner daringly changed that by wearing a dress that matched his outfit. Their idea that pair teams should present a unified look became the style that continues today.

As a competitive skater, Vera attracted attention along with gold medals and saw her achievements featured in *Sports Illustrated* and the *New York Times*.

Vera worked hard to reach the top level of her sport while also continuing to earn top grades in school. Some skaters going for their Olympic dreams would drop out of school and get private tutors so they could train harder. They would even leave their families and move to other cities and states to live with strangers, if that was what it took to get more ice time and better coaches. "I always seemed to be thrust into this world where the bar was so high," Vera recalled in later years. "I am the first child in my family to survive, and a lot of pressure was put on me. I remember saying, 'Mom, I can't compete if I'm skating half the time that other skaters skate.'"

When Vera made the case for dropping all other activities, including school, so she could devote more time to skating, Florence pointed out that great skaters like Dick Button and Tenley Albright had won Olympic medals without dropping out of school. In fact, she always told Vera, Albright went on to graduate from Harvard and become a surgeon, while Button also graduated from both Harvard and law school before becoming a sports commentator. Vera could not convince her parents that figure skating had gotten intensely more competitive.

The pressure remained heavy on Vera. In addition to her challenging school, her training and other activities, she was being groomed by her parents to become a debutante. Being a debutante follows an old tradition for young ladies of the upper classes and aristocracy to be formally introduced during a series of balls. This marked the passage of their teenage daughters formally "coming out" into society. Vera made her debut in late 1968. As a mark of her charisma in a sea of other beautiful young debs, the *New York Times* chose Vera's picture to splash across its pages chronicling the debutante ball. The paper quoted Vera saying she was only doing the debutante duty to please her parents. She also revealed she was not in the market for a potential husband.

Vera finally convinced her parents to allow her to drop out of the Chapin School before her final year started in September so she could train for the 1968 Olympics, only months away. Vera's timing, however, was bad. She came of age in the sport at the same time as Peggy Fleming, who was a year older. Fleming is one of the greatest women figure skaters of all time. She also had the critical experience of having competed in international competitions, including the 1964 Olympics. Fleming's parents had uprooted the entire family so she could train in Colorado. She looked unbeatable, and would ultimately prove to be unbeatable.

Vera competed against Fleming in the 1968 National Championships—the winners would be placed on the Olympic team. Fleming won.

Debutantes from Texas practice their curtsy during the Fifty-fourth International Debutante Ball at the Waldorf-Astoria hotel in 2008 in New York. The debutantes included European aristocrats and scions of American families from the Social Register.

Peggy Fleming, American figure skater, preparing for a gold medal bid in figure skating at the 1968 Winter Olympics at Grenoble, France.

The 1968 Olympics

At the 1968 Olympics in Grenoble, France, Peggy Fleming earned the only gold medal for America in the entire games. She became a hero. The combination of her appeal and mix of grace with athleticism showed all that is great about the sport. She reaped the benefit of the new satellite technology that allowed for the first time for the Olympics to be broadcast live, or close to, when the events were happening, giving excitement to the audience that previous skating coverage had lacked.

Viewers saw an elegant young woman in a green dress, and it sparked America's love affair with figure skating. Fleming became such a huge star she got her own television series of specials. Four different presidential administrations invited her to the White House. The plain green dress that her mother had made for her was placed in the Smithsonian museum where great American treasures preside, like Dorothy's ruby slippers from *The Wizard of Oz*.

To the Wangs, it wasn't about Peggy Fleming's greatness. It was about Vera's loss. "When I didn't make the (Olympic) team, my parents were horrified." It didn't matter that there are tens of thousands of children skating across ice rinks year after year, and only a handful of them ever make it to the world-class level. To expect their daughter to skate up to the standards of Peggy Fleming shows how high the bar was set in the Wang household. Vera was expected to achieve at the highest levels.

3

Pairing Up

Despite her upsetting defeat, Vera still didn't give up on her Olympic dreams.

There are three kinds of figure skating categories: pair skating, ice dancing, and singles skating (with male and female divisions). As a singles skater, Vera competed in two events required at each competition in those days: free skating with its jumps and spins set to music, and the school figures (the figure eights that give the sport its name.) As a detail-oriented athlete, she excelled in the exacting school figures, which helped her make it to the championships year after year. In the free skate portion, her ballet training and determination helped her become a strong competitor as well. Then in her teen years she took on another challenge, training as a pairs skater with partner James Stuart. This meant even more practice time.

Vera was finding it too difficult to balance schoolwork and skating. She wanted to achieve excellence in all her activities, but there wasn't enough time to do it all and go to college, too. She had to get even stronger in her upper body to hold the

Vera's Olympic dreams were dashed as her partner decided to quit pairs skating. Pictured is the general stadium for the 1972 Winter Olympics in Sapporo, Japan.

positions in the lifts as she would be carried high over her partner's head across the ice. Pairs skaters feature "throw jumps" where the man literally throws the woman into the air as she performs a double axel or other jumps. That means the woman has to have the strength to hold a jumping position from five and six feet in the air and come down securely on a steel blade only one quarter inch thick.

Vera and Jimmy trained hard, and qualified for the 1969 Nationals Championships. From there, they aimed to compete in the World Figure Skating Championships and maybe even the next Olympics, in 1972.

At Nationals they took fifth place. But Jimmy announced that he wanted to quit pairs and gamble on making it as a singles skater. Vera was devastated. She found herself without a partner, and it was too late to make up for lost ground and go back to competing as a singles skater. Just like that, her skating career was over. For as long as she could remember what got her out of bed every morning before dawn was the dream of becoming a world champion. Now that goal was gone. She was nineteen.

After she quit skating, Vera needed a new goal. Her father wanted her to become a doctor or lawyer, and she started out to fulfill his wishes. She knew she had the discipline to withstand the intense demands of medical school.

She enrolled at Sarah Lawrence College, near her Manhattan home. But without skating, she felt like a boat that had lost its anchor. She could not make herself stay in school. This was the turning point in her life.

"During this time I had a breakdown," Wang recalled. "I dropped out of Sarah Lawrence College. I didn't feel I was achieving anything. The emptiness I experienced is what I now know is depression—but I didn't know that when I was 19. People didn't talk openly about depression in 1969.

You don't know you're depressed; you just know your life doesn't feel right. I know I represented a huge disappointment to my parents. They said it in a million ways every day, never outright, but it was conveyed to me in so many ways."

As she said later, "I had to learn a big life lesson, which is that when you are so obsessed by something and you can no longer do it, you dust yourself off and keep going.

Wang shocked her parents by dropping out of her college premed studies. Then she shocked them even more by announcing that she was moving to Paris. She had become romantically involved with a French ice skating champion she had known in the small, tight-knit skating world, Patrick Pera.

In Paris, Vera's boyfriend was the toast of the town. He had won a bronze medal in the 1968 Olympics and was still competing and winning honors for his country. He would go on to win silver medal in the 1971 World Championships.

Vera loved the pace of life in Paris. She enrolled in the Sorbonne, one of the world's best universities. She loved the university as much as she did the city. She also realized what she loved above all else was art. This realization gave her a new goal. After two years in Europe, she returned home a much wiser and more independent and worldly woman. It was 1970 and she was twenty-one years old.

Back home in the United States, Vera re-enrolled in Sarah Lawrence and earned her bachelor of arts degree in art history. After graduation, she began pursuing another passion—fashion. "With the end of my skating career, there was a sense of loss and failure, a lack of passion and a questioning of what I was doing in my life. So I replaced skating with the best of fashion. And ever since, I've tried to stay focused on what I want to do and what brings me a sense of self-worth and dignity," she said. "My passion is what I need to do to feel healthy and sane and like I'm making a contribution in some small way. That's what drives me."

Wang approached her parents with her decision to pursue fashion instead of medicine or the law. Her father refused to

Sorbonne University, Paris, France

spend any of his considerable wealth on what he saw as frippery. Although he and his wife believed in investing in the finest things, and they loved fashionable clothing, he saw the design profession as unworthy of his oldest child. She had a strong mind and first-class education. He did not want to see her devote her life to a career he thought was trivial.

Wang found herself at another crossroads. She wanted to honor her traditional upbringing, to honor her father's wishes. But she knew in her heart he was wrong. It stung that he did not have confidence in her. "He thought the chances of me making it as a designer were, like, less than zero. He said, 'Listen, I paid for five years of undergraduate. How about law school or business school? Go to Yale Law.' I said nope. And then, I think just to make me really aggravated, he said, "I'm not paying for anything else.'"

Wang rebelled. She had taken a summer job as a shop-girl working at the Yves St. Laurent boutique in New York, one of her mother's favorite French designers, when she was in college. She had worked hard, and cultivated influential people

YVES SAINT LAURENT
rive gauche
YVES SAINT LAURENT
rive gauche
YVES SAINT LAURENT
rive gauche

Yves St. Laurent's boutique in Milan.
He was a favorite designer of Wang's mother, Florence.

who shopped there. Although she had been raised to honor traditional Asian cultural practices, she was also a New Yorker, a person comfortable in a crowd, her voice strong and bold and her manner supremely confident.

"I knew the world I wanted to be in, but I wasn't sure I could break into that world. My mother was an incredible clotheshorse, so I grew up loving fashion. I lived in Paris during my junior and senior years at Sarah Lawrence. When you're in Paris, you can't help but notice fashion. I wanted something to do with fashion. I would have done anything. I would have swept floors. I would have licked envelopes. I just wanted to be part of it."

Wang discovered she liked working with customers and that she was truly gifted at helping women choose fashions that looked great on them. Her artist's eye guided her to inspired color combinations that flattered her customers' skin tone. She met many wealthy and powerful women, and one who took a liking to her was Frances Patiky Stein. Stein was an editor at *Vogue.* The magazine was the most powerful in the fashion industry. Stein had taken a liking to Wang's smarts and suggested she give her a call when she graduated.

A few years later Wang took Stein up on the offer. She called her, got herself an interview, and talked her way into a job at *Vogue.* Her first job was an entry-level post as an assistant. She worked long hours doing menial work. She raced around taking care of the thousands of little details and errands that make the photos look so elegant and effortless. Wang was determined that she would show her father she could make it on her own.

On her first day of work she showed up in a favorite Yves St. Laurent outfit she hoped would impress her new boss. They took one look at her and sent her home to change, telling her that her job was to do the dirty work. She happily returned in jeans, and loved rolling up her sleeves.

"I come from a wealthy family, but I'm a working girl from a working family," said Wang. "I don't want to be viewed as a dilettante. I have a very real picture of what money is. If you come from a family that's made money you know more about its value than those who have never had it."

Wang's first fashion job was an entry level position at *Vogue*.
Vogue covers on Champs-Elysees, Paris, France

VOGUE

APRIL 15
50p

HOW TO
DRESS
MAKE-UP
TRAVEL
EAT
LIVE
WITH

MORE
DASH
THAN
CASH

PLUS
MEN IN
VOGUE

4

Oh So *Vogue*

For sixteen years Wang had worked her way up the ladder at *Vogue*, putting in long hours and hard word. "*Vogue* is a seductive place because of what you get to see and what you're privy to; it's a world that I can't even explain," said Wang. "I thought I would do it for a year or two and I ended up staying 16 years. During that time, I rose to be one of the youngest editors ever in the history of *Vogue*. By twenty-three, I was a senior editor, and then I became European editor for American *Vogue* in Paris."

What she loved best was seeing fashion designers at work. She studied their creative process, with the advantage of seeing it with a bigger-picture perspective of a journalist. Wang was going for the gold medal in fashion. She aimed for nothing less than becoming editor of *Vogue*.

But despite her hard work, Wang's dream did not come true—again. She found herself bypassed in 1985, when the editor's job went to Anna Wintour. Wintour is considered so formidable that she has held the very demanding and powerful chief editor's position for more than twenty-five years

Ralph Lauren's Bleecker Street store in
Greenwich Village in Manhattan

and is said to be the model for the best-selling book and hit Hollywood movie *The Devil Wears Prada*.

Wang then went to work for designer Ralph Lauren. At Lauren, she worked hard for two years and learned a great deal about the classic American styling that is Lauren's specialty. She served as a design director, overseeing thirteen accessory lines. Wang was designing lingerie and sportswear at a time when aerobics dance classes and jazzercise were becoming a major trend. For Wang, her job experience was the equivalent of earning a graduate degree on how to be a fashion designer. Now she felt she was ready to graduate.

5

The World of Romance

orking for Ralph Lauren gave Wang time for romance in her life. She had met Arthur Becker, a stockbroker at the Wall Street firm of Bear, Stearns & Co., at a tennis match in 1980. Arthur was handsome, intelligent, and he made her laugh. He too had grown up with a strong and independent mother and a hard-charging and successful father.

Becker hadn't made much of an impression on her at their first meeting. Nevertheless, he persisted, and in 1988 they became engaged. Their engagement announcement and their wedding were featured prominently in the *New York Times*.

Wang's biggest disappointment during the planning of her wedding was the search for a gown. She saw only dresses she thought lacked imagination and style. As she tried them on and looked in the mirror, she felt as uninspired as the empty-headed plastic doll that traditionally decorated wedding cakes. She decided to design her own dress and found seamstresses talented enough to execute her design.

Wang and Becker were married at the elegant Pierre
Hotel near Central Park in Manhattan.

For a fabric she chose white duchesse satin, which would become a staple for her. She created a hand-beaded white gown with a full skirt. Her dress cost $10,000 and weighed forty-five pounds. The heavy weight of the gown would later propel her into searching for a glamorous but lightweight fabric for her designs. She knew firsthand what it felt like to look like a dream but move like an elephant in such a gown.

The couple married on June 22, 1989, just days before her fortieth birthday, in a lavish celebration. The guest list topped four hundred and a twenty-five piece orchestra entertained the crowd filling a ballroom in the elegant Pierre Hotel on Central Park. Her ceremony was a mix of two cultures and religions, Christian and Judaism. Both a Baptist minister and a rabbi performed the ceremonies.

In the Chinese culture, custom calls for the bride to change clothes during different parts of the festivities. For her reception Wang chose a simple pink slip dress.

Six months after her wedding, Wang quit working at *Vogue*. She and Becker wanted to start a family immediately, and Wang worried the stress of her job might interfere with her ability to conceive. But even without the stress of work, Wang failed to get pregnant. She turned to fertility treatments. However, the daily medical grind of shots and tests, coupled with the mood swings from the hormones, took a toll on her.

While one aspect of Wang's life seemed uncertain, in other ways her life was progressing. Her father approached her and suggested the time was ripe for her to start her own fashion design business. He had remembered how frustrated she became when she couldn't find a suitable wedding gown, and he saw an important opening in the market that he believed his daughter could fill.

He proposed backing her financially. Wang turned him down at first; she had waited for decades for him to say those words, but felt it was too late. C. C. Wang persisted, saying that since she would no longer be as emotional about this business,

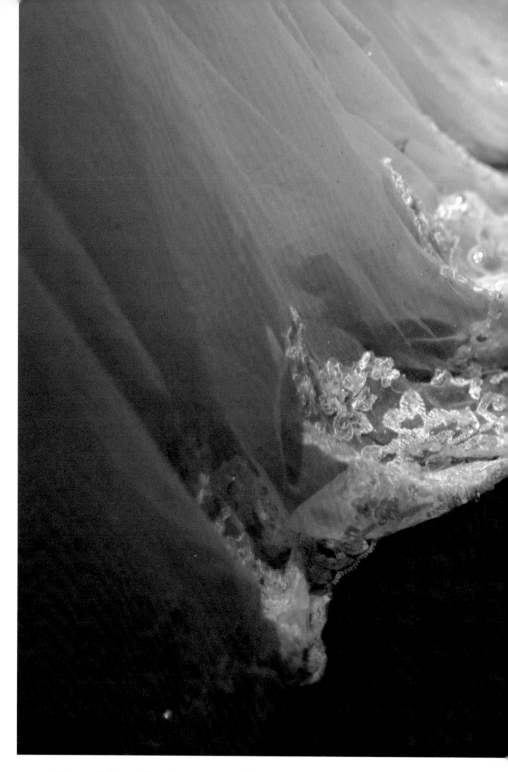

The search for wedding dresses is what first launched Wang into her successful design business.

she therefore would approach it with more clear thinking and have a better chance at success.

Meanwhile, Wang and Becker realized they wouldn't be able to conceive their own children even with the help of medical science. They decided to adopt. Their first child was a biracial girl named Cecilia, whose parents were European and Asian. She was born in 1990, and came home with them in 1991. Wang felt very keenly the duality of being a child from two different cultures, and she felt excitement about being able to offer the best of both worlds to her daughter. The couple named their second daughter Josephine.

Wang decided to enter the fashion business. Her father would serve as her financial adviser, and she would design the wedding gowns.

At first Wang thought she had no interest in wedding gowns. She had designed her own when she couldn't find one she liked for her wedding, but had not thought of making wedding gowns as a business opportunity. But it was a way to reenter a business she loved, and Wang determined to make it a success. Besides, her father had challenged her and she took the challenge. He invested $4 million and became her first, and only, investor.

Vera Wang greets the audience after her collection of bridal wear was modeled in New York, 2007

The Vera Wang Spring 2009 collection

6

Ripping Out the Seams of Tradition

C. Wang had chosen wisely for his daughter. Weddings are a $60 billion a year industry. Wang thought that twentieth-century bridal gowns had grown to look like wedding cakes—big puffy layer upon layer of white leading up to the narrow upper layer across the chest, which were always done up in white lace. She thought they resembled Little Bo Peep without the sheep.

However, when it came to wedding dresses tradition ruled. Wang knew she had her work cut out for her if she was going to change what brides wanted on their wedding day.

Wang's first step was to decide where to set up her shop. She didn't want to open a bridal store. Her salon had to be different, more theatrical than the usual wedding shop. She knew her prospective customers, because they were wealthy people like herself.

Wang decided to open her wedding gown boutique in the exclusive Carlyle Hotel in Manhattan's tony Upper East Side, the neighborhood where she had grown up. A two-story

A view of the lake in Central Park.

salon, the doors stayed locked. Only those with appointments gain entry.

At first, Wang sold gowns by other designers as she prepared to start selling her own custom-made gowns. Because of the sheer size and amount of fabric used in wedding dresses, they take an enormous amount of time to cut and assemble and decorate by hand.

Wang was not going to open just another bridal shop. Determined to only make gowns for people who could afford the finest, she tripled or even quadrupled the current top-end price of wedding gowns. If women would pay $5,000 for a traditional Little Bo Peep style, she thought, imagine what kind of gown they could get for $15,000, or $25,000? She used her fashion pedigree as a former *Vogue* insider to impress potential customers with her sense of style, fitting expertise, and ability to take all these thousands of details off the already overwhelming to-do list of the bride.

Vera Wang Bridal House opened in 1990. Not limiting herself totally to wedding gowns, across the street she opened Vera Wang Made to Order salon, where she created custom-made dresses and evening wear. Business was slow at first because she was so untraditional. But she got a big boost from her friends at *Vogue*, who were on the same wavelength about wedding fashions desperately needing a makeover. The magazine did a big spread about her new boutique. This gave her important buzz among the fashionable set. Said Wang of her new venture:

> Our kind of bridal salon didn't exist before. I wanted a comfortable residential environment. And for the price of one retail dress you get a lot of attention plus all the accessories right there, and advice on everything, even flowers, and no consulting fee. I wanted to be exclusive by taste, not money. Small and caring. I look at every dress in the store. I had a whole glove line made up that didn't exist. And I was thinking wouldn't it be nice to take off your shoes, have a Diet Coke and not be bride No. 5,076 for the month of June.

Since her approach to weddings was new and nontraditional, it took time to catch on. It was scary for Wang, after years of being part of a team, to suddenly be performing solo again. She remained acutely aware of the costs and initial investment. For the first time she had employees relying

Vera Wang applauds her models after a showing of
Wang's wedding fashions May, 2001.

on her. To make matters more stressful, the American economy was in a recession in 1990.

Luckily, she found a great partner, Chet Hazzard, who she had met while working at *Vogue*. After two years of renovating and decorating the two-story boutique and getting the business on solid financial ground they had slowly built a loyal client base. The word was getting around to more and more of the elite that Vera Wang Bridal House was the in-place to get a custom-made wedding gown.

When Wang and Hazzard looked for fabric suppliers, they couldn't find any that met their high standards. They worked with delicate and expensive white fabrics that could not be around any machine that used oil. Frustrated at not being able to find suitable fabric, they opened their own factories in Florida and in Ohio.

Hazzard said, "We're prudent people. . . . We didn't show (our clothing collections in runway fashion shows) for the first five years. We built our own factories instead. . . . We built our factories like pharmaceutical plants. Impeccable." Once completed, they took great care to run the factories well.

Wang knew that the secret to her success was providing excellent service. When people can afford whatever they want, when price is not an issue, what matters most is great service. She made sure her employees were all gracious and well-mannered. Fine drink and food was served to prospective customers. Not only was Wang selling wedding gowns, she wanted to make certain that during the wedding preparations, which is often a highly stressful time, her shop was a relaxing oasis.

Wang remained conscientious about not being pushy or forcing her product on customers. She learned the wedding world is fraught with expectations, the fantasies of little girls now grown up that they wanted to come true. She proceeded diplomatically.

"For most women, a wedding gown represents far more than just a dress. It is also the embodiment of a dream. This fantasy of idealized happiness, the groom represents perfection and the face of all human possibility," Wang said.

When she greets a new client, Wang draws out the details of their event. Is the ceremony in daytime or at night? Is it in a hotel, church, restaurant, or tent? How many people are attending? The details then dictate how a dress needs to be designed to fit in. From the facts she then works to marry the bride's reality with her fantasy.

In the early days, when business was slow, she worried about how to keep her staff and seamstresses busy. Then she had an "Aha" moment. She would have them stitch dresses for bridesmaids, flower girls, and little tuxes and tails for the ring bearers. When she couldn't find gloves that fit her vision of the perfect wedding glove, she designed her own. Then she moved slowly step-by-step to other pieces of the bridal ensemble. Not just any white shoe will do with a wedding dress. The veils and the headdresses also didn't fit in with her modern

The Vera Wang spring
2009 collection

designs, so she created new styles to complement her gowns. Eventually, she was designing everything from the lingerie to the dress the bride wore to the reception.

The business was growing and doing very well when a terrible tragedy struck. In 1994, armed robbers burst into her wedding salon and mugged the parents of a bride who had come to choose a gown for the happiest day of her life. When the parents didn't move fast enough, the robbers shot them in the stomach and fled. The criminals were later caught, tried, and imprisoned. It was devastating to Wang and her fledgling business. But the public demand for her services continued, and her business flourished despite the tragic event.

Wang became immersed in weddings and decided she wanted to share her expertise and advise to women who could not afford her services. She created an elaborate over-sized book about everything from gloves to ring bearers to napkin rings. The book answered an array of questions for all types of wedding. Readers learned, for example, that the neckline of the flower girl's dress should always be modest. The book included tips for second-time brides, military brides, and gay brides. Her main point was that "the dress should suit the occasion and complement the wearer." She urges brides to talk frankly about identity and religion, to discuss where they will live, and especially talk about money with their future husbands.

To ensure her book met her high expectations, she wrote it all herself and handled much of its publication. She wanted it to look exactly as she thought it should. It needed to uphold the Wang standards. Published in September 2001, she also wrote frankly about her own life and wedding, intertwined with her details and information about how to approach weddings and choose the perfect dress and service. She jokes that she launched a business soon after her own wedding and never had time to assemble the photographs into a proper wedding album. This book, she said, would serve as her wedding album.

Later, when the Internet began to develop, she created a Web site that offers even more information and tips. It also includes sample gown styles and photos and videos.

"If I were to listen to many other voices I would have done a safe product," Wang reflected. "Would anyone believe that a Sheer Illusion low-cut-back slinky dress would ever have sold in the bridal market? Ten out of ten people would say you are out of your mind. I said there have to be women like me who are not 23 and want to look sophisticated and sexy. And if I don't do it nobody else will give them an alternative."

Nancy Kerrigan performs during the technical program portion of the
1994 Olympic women's figure skating competition.

7

Olympic Dreams: The Triumphant Sequel

er life had shaped into an exciting whirl of roles: mother, wife, entrepreneur, author, and artist. As though this was not enough Vera Wang decided to again become involved in Olympic figure skating.

Her involvement began in 1991 when an old acquaintance from her skating days approached her about designing competition dresses. Wang had known Mary Batdorf and her twin sister, Anne, from the tight-knit world of figure skating. Now thirty years later Mary was married to another skating pro named Evy Scotvold. They trained young skaters and Mary wanted a knockout skating outfit for their student, Nancy Kerrigan, who would be competing in the 1992 Olympics in France.

Kerrigan's chief rivals were younger and more athletic skaters. The Scotvolds wanted Kerrigan to project a more sophisticated appearance to give her an edge. Mary was a stylish woman with class, and she loved Wang's evening wear. She had approached Wang because she knew as a former skater, she would understand the mechanics of movement that an ice skating dress would need to withstand as much as wear as a running shoe but look as fabulous as an evening gown.

A dress worthy of Olympians looks deceptively simpler than it is in reality. Skaters whip across the ice so fast the outfit has to be able to resist nearly high pressure. It can't ride up on the crotch or the wrists or plunge too low in the neck. (One famous competitor had her breast pop out of her low-cut dress while leaning forward during a camel spin during a performance.) It has to look sensational from the back as well as the front and side because the skater is always changing direction and being photographed from all angles.

If the skater falls and scrambles to get up it can't restrict her movements or leave a wet stain from the ice that highlights the mistake. The material must stretch like yoga pants but look stunning as an Oscar dress. If it's adorned with beads and trim, they must be secured and not pop off, for even the tiniest bit of fluff can get caught in the blades of a speeding skater and pose danger. It must catch the audience imagination but not look tacky and match the music and the mood. A deep red tango style dress wouldn't suit a program to peppy Broadway show tunes.

Wang relished the technical challenge and loved the nostalgia of revisiting her love for ice skating. "You can't believe the technology and handwork that go into these little bitty dresses," she said. "You have a tiny surface to make a fashion statement, and everything has to fit like a second skin. This isn't some dress you're going to stand around in at a cocktail party. It has to survive a flying sit spin."

Wang's design became a breakthrough in the world of skating. The dress highlighted the elegance of Kerrigan's style. Glowing white with sheer sleeves also in white, the body of the dress and skirt were made of a solid, stretchy fabric. The front resembled the classical design of a Grecian urn, cut into a V shape that ended in a halter style around the neck. The skirt fluttered as delicate as a bird as she zipped across the ice.

Nancy Kerrigan, performs at the 1992 World Figure Skating Championships in Oakland, California.

At the Olympics the media gushed with stories praising the dress as a welcome relief from the other competitors' outfits. Some skaters were wearing feathers, others showing embarrassing amounts of flesh. Skating authorities started setting rules banning styles they found offensive. Both Wang and Kerrigan were a hit and credited with setting a new standard that put class back on ice.

But Wang's first skating dress lost points on a technicality. Kerrigan complained about it afterward, saying it didn't stretch enough for her to be able to get the proper windup for her triple lutz (one of the hardest triple jumps, with three revolutions in the air.) "When you're skating, the last thing you want to think about is, 'My costume is killing me! 'You want to be able to think only about what you have trained for and what you need to do."

Kerrigan came in third. American Kristi Yamaguchi won the gold medal. Kerrigan placed one spot ahead another American teammate, Tanya Harding.

For the 1994 Winter Olympics in Norway, Mary Scotvold and Nancy Kerrigan again came calling on Vera Wang. In the intervening two years, helped with the heaps of positive free publicity from her first Olympics dress, Wang had become hot property. Her wedding designs had grown more varied and her evening wear was getting attention especially from Hollywood actresses. This time, team Kerrigan turned to Wang's evening gowns for inspiration.

For one of her performance dresses, Wang argued with Kerrigan to drop the pastels the skater preferred. Too bland, Wang advised. They settled on a powerful almost neon yellow sleeveless dress that filled the ice and made Kerrigan look electrifying.

For Kerrigan's short program, Wang created a white dress with black velvet inserts that looked classic and poised. It was adapted from Wang's ready-to-wear collection from the high-end department store Barney's New York and featured

U.S. Olympic figure
skater Nancy Kerrigan,
February, 1994

sheer sleeves edged at the wrists with rhinestones and pearls. Kerrigan skated to the top in it.

Wang saved her masterpiece for Kerrigan's long and final program. Dubbed the Golden Illusion dress, it was made out of lightweight fabric sewn with 11,500 rhinestones. The jewels were heat-pressed onto the surface of the fabric so it wouldn't be weighed down with metal or stitching. Otherwise it would weigh so much Kerrigan couldn't take off for those jumps. The light it projected lit up Kerrigan's own beauty. It was adapted from an evening gown Wang had designed for actress Sharon Stone, her friend and one of her earliest celebrity customers. Stone had started turning heads wearing Vera Wang's gowns for major awards ceremonies like the Oscars and started a trend of celebrities from Hollywood and beyond to choose Wang's flattering and subtly different designs.

The price tag on this Olympic mini-gown was staggering, $13,000. Wang donated the competition dresses to Kerrigan along with the $9,000 white-on-black dress. "It's one of my favorite dresses," Kerrigan said. "The kids at my rink where I train told me they kept watching the dress instead of me because it looks so amazing."

But then a bizarre turn of events almost kept Wang's creations from seeing the light of day. In January 1994, in advance of the National Figure Skating Championships in Detroit, Michigan, Nancy Kerrigan left the ice during a practice session. A stranger sidled up to her and asked for her autograph. In the crush of people they ended up behind a curtain near the rink and then suddenly people heard Kerrigan shriek in pain. The strange man had kneecapped her, striking a blow across her knees with a heavy metal rod before fleeing. She cried out, "Why me? Why, why why?"

The assailant turned out to be connected with Kerrigan's rival ice skating competitor, Tonya Harding. What unfolded was one of the most tawdry episodes ever to hit figure skating. Harding was a tough competitor, but her life was not as tidy as her skating. The scandal consumed the media and the public. What did Tanya know? Was she in on it?

Nancy Kerrigan gives a silver medal performance in the women's free skating program in 1994.

Should she be allowed to compete? Would Kerrigan recover in time to compete? Would she ever recover, for the knees of an ice skater were the most important body part. The debate raged. Women's figure skating became major news, and it was not pretty.

Without Kerrigan competing, Harding won Nationals, and second place went to a very young Michelle Kwan. Technically, they should have been named as the Olympic team. The international skating federation however was stumped. Soon it came out that Harding had known of the attack, and it had been planned by her husband and an associate. The skating authorities didn't want to reward Harding if she was guilty, but it was too soon to determine. The Olympics were only weeks away in Lillehammer, Norway. So the authorities granted Kerrigan a bypass to the Games and allowed Harding to compete. At the last minute, they sent as an alternate Michelle Kwan, a Chinese American skater from California who was only thirteen years old, but a dazzling skater already.

When it came time to unveil the Vera Wang dress, there was so much media focused on the Olympics and ladies figure skating that the press was there in force. They had to have something to write about. So they wrote about Nancy Kerrigan's dresses. Like everything else with this drama, it was definitely different. People were tired of the nasty turn of events, and the dresses provided something beautiful to focus on.

With Kerrigan's dark hair and classy skating style, the gold dress dazzled. Wang did not miscalculate. For Kerrigan, it seemed as if she had slipped into her glass slipper—she skated the best program of her career.

Kerrigan did not win the gold metal that Olympics. She had to deal with so much stress, the pressure, the spotlight, the injury, and the tension she felt having to practice on the same ice as Harding. While Kerrigan performed brilliantly, the crowd favorite proved to be a Ukrainian orphan who had suffered much tragedy in her short life, Oksana Bayul.

Nancy Kerrigan, center, talks to her coach Mary Scotvold as teammate Tonya Harding, right, skates by during the first Olympic practice session together for the two American skaters in February 1994, in Hamar, Norway.

Nancy Kerrigan performing during a Winter
Olympic exhibition in Hamar, Norway.
Kerrigan took home the silver medal in the
women's figure skating competition.

Oksana performed even more brilliantly and added more difficult jumps to capture the gold. It didn't matter. Kerrigan finished the game a superstar, and so did Vera Wang.

The fashion of ice skating became such big business that one fashion newspaper, *Women's Wear Daily*, hired Wang to "cover" the 2002 Winter Olympics in Salt Lake City, Utah, as a fashion journalist. More dresses would follow for more Olympians, including Kwan. In 2010 Wang got back on the ice again to design for leading men's figure skating competitor Evan Lysacek for the Olympics in Vancouver, Canada. He stood at the top of the awards podium at the Olympics as they hung the gold medal around the neck of his Vera Wang outfit. She had her Olympic gold in a way she never dreamed of.

Designer Vera Wang
ponders a reporter's
question during an
interview in her studio.

8

Brand Vera

By the middle of the 1990s it seemed that anytime there was a red carpet parade of celebrities, there was a Vera Wang gown. Her designs appeared at all the big Hollywood events. Wang dressed Sharon Stone, Holly Hunter, and Patty Scalfia, the stylish rock star wife of rocker Bruce Springsteen. For entertainer Mariah Carey she created a dazzling wedding gown with a twenty-seven-foot-long train. Wang dressed celebrity Jennifer Lopez for weddings—twice.

As a businesswoman, Wang has been innovative, quality-conscious, and aggressive about expansion. She has taken her business opportunities global. She branched into all aspects of the weddings. In 1995 she opened Maids on Madison, specializing in bridesmaid dresses as well as ensembles for attendants and flower girls. By 1995 her retail operations earned about $10 million per year and her fame was still growing. Her bridal and evening wear were being sold at such exclusive shops as Barney's, Neiman Marcus, and Saks Fifth Avenue. She opened another full-scale bridal salon in Washington, D.C.

Vera Wang's perfume is fashioned after classic French scents.

In 2000, Wang released perfumes to wear on the wedding day. It took her years to negotiate a deal with the international corporation Unilever, makers of personal care products and food such as Ben & Jerry's premium ice cream. Wang wanted to create a perfume that expressed the ideal of romance. Her goal was to deliver a fragrance for women who might not be able to afford her bridal designs but still wanted to capture some of Wang's now-famous romantic ideals. Over the years she has created ten fragrances with other companies as well: Vera Wang, Sheer Veil, Truly Pink, Princess, Rock Princess, Glam Princess, Flower Princess (inspired by her daughters), Look, Bouquet, and Vera Wang for Men.

Wang's first licensing deal, with an Italian shoe company named Rossimoda, was for a shoe with a narrow platform heel to provide a longer line and the appearance of being taller and thinner. They came in satin, velvet, and suede. Wang was also proud to carry the first license for the legendary Waterford Wedgwood China and crystal makers. It was the first licensing arrangement for that United Kingdom company for centuries.

By 2001 Wang was selling 10,000 custom-made dresses a year. The future looked good—especially in Vera Wang eyeglasses, her newest licensing venture. She kept expanding into home collection, plates, china, tableware, vases, and wine goblets. Wang changed her shoe designer to Stuart Weitzman, with Wang designing the shoes and Weitzman producing and distributing them. She changed in order to have more shoes produced faster to keep up with demand. Later, she partnered with another Italian designer, Giuseppe Zanotti, and their first collection appeared in 2004.

Wang manages to stay fresh enough in her designs to attract A-list celebrities. She admits she still gets a charge out of seeing her designs on women walking down the street, or in the spotlight on the red carpet on TV. Among her fans are actresses Alicia Silverstone, Halle Barry, Renee Zellwegger, and Reese Witherspoon. Wang dressed First Lady Hillary Rodham Clinton, who chose Vera Wang gowns for many

President and Hillary Clinton, wearing a Vera Wang designed gown, greet Chinese President Jiang Zemin and his wife Wang Yeping prior to a state dinner in the Chinese president's honor in October 1997.

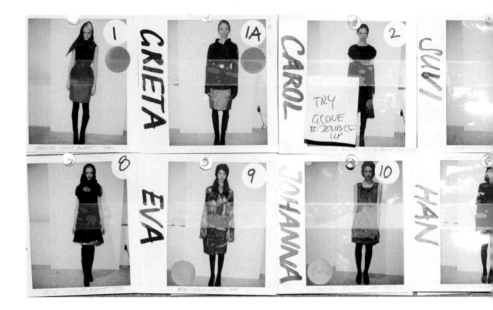

special occasions while in the White House. Wang and her husband Arthur Becker became good friends with Hillary and her husband, President Bill Clinton.

Vera Wang has achieved a name for creating a signature look of clean lines, luxurious materials and uncomplicated sophisticated gowns. "The magic [of making a gown fit well] is in weightless cloth, treating beading as texture, cutting arm-holes that add grace," she said. "Cleverly exposing the best parts and sensuously draping fabric over less fabulous ones, offering enough internal support to allow a woman freedom to show off while being totally comfortable. Because a woman is never sexier than when she's comfortable in her clothes."

As a woman raised in two divergent cultures, Vera Wang entered her sixth decade of life having successfully combined her traditional Asian upbringing with can-do spirit of her native country, America.

In business, Wang has successfully married art and commerce. She has been critically acclaimed and has earned great

financial reward. She presides as chief executive officer and sole owner of an international corporation constantly growing and profitable.

In her personal life Wang balances motherhood with career, marriage, work, and philanthropy. She has devoted much time and talent to charities. Among her efforts include work to benefit those suffering from AIDS. She lost her wonderful and much loved partner, Chet Hazzard, to complications from AIDS in 2005. She contributed to helping the victims of the September 11, 2001, terrorist attacks on New York City, her hometown, as well as Pennsylvania and Washington, D.C. Wang also took part with others in the fashion industry to assist victims of the deadly Hurricane Katrina, which wreaked devastation across four southern states and left millions uprooted and suffering.

In business, Wang continues to develop and find new markets, new niches, and new fields to conquer including the Vera Wang Fine Jewelry line sold in her own signature boutiques.

Wang surrounds herself with inspirational art in her studio.

Goddess of Romantic Style

Perhaps Vera Wang should take the nickname Venus, after the Roman goddess of love. For she seems to have cornered the market on all the most romantic parts of weddings.

Wang started her empire with satin and lace. From the purity of white satin gowns for blushing brides, she moved even into the more sensual side of romance. She designed lingerie. Then in 2005, only fifteen years later, she unveiled her most expensive design undertaking so far, the Vera Wang Suite in romantic Hawaii.

Wang considers Hawaii one of the most beautiful places on earth. "As in fashion, a luxury resort creates an aesthetic and emotional experience. This is what I wanted to capture," said Wang.

The suite is more than 2,000 square feet. Throughout its light-filled interior she strove for elegance and understatement—the musical equivalent of a string quartet instead of a full symphony. There are no hot tubs in the shape of a champagne glass and other honeymoon-oriented gimmicks some hotels like to promote.

All this glorious luxury comes with a world-class price tag: it costs more than $4,000 a night to stay there. But there is no other place like the Vera Wang suite. It is not unique for fashion designers to lend their flair to hotel design, the few who enter this realm design full hotels. Vera created simply one sumptuous suite.

The room that bears her name offers the privacy of the second floor of the Halekulani Hotel overlooking Honolulu's legendary Waikiki Beach. The hotel has long been a resort with roots stretching back nearly ninety years. It offers a long lanai, or patio, that looks out upon the Pacific Ocean and Diamond Head volcano. The volcano's soaring peak is breathtaking and the most famous landmark of the islands. From the balcony the gentle sounds of the ocean can be heard.

The decor has contrasting textures and colors and an Asian, tropical theme. The room is scented with arrangements of tropical flowers. Greeting visitors is a serene stone statue of Quan Yin, a feminine incarnation of Buddha who according to ancient Chinese tradition welcomes travelers at the gate and transforms the experience from travel to serenity.

The walls are not painted but covered in soft white cloth. In contrast she has done the floor in a solid dark tropical wood called Wenge. The hotel room has a dining room with a table also made out of the tropical Wenge, with a lighter-shade of chairs from cane. The living room offers color to liven up the dark wood and soft white walls. It features bright tropical colors and deep sofas in her favorite color, purple. She mixes old with new objects from around the world. The bedroom has warm relaxing neutral tones with side tables made from rare palm wood and a mirror over the bed, that catches the reflection of the Hawaiian sunrise.

Couples dine on Vera Wang china, crystal, and forks and knives—all from Vera Wang's home collection. The pillows on the couches use fabric from her dresses. Included with the room comes champagne, a limousine, and a private butler service.

Following Wang's favorite design themes of mixing up textures her suite does the same, all of them muted and luxurious. On the floor she has placed coarse hemp rugs the color of khaki pants.

The bathroom is enormous—with a toilet seat lid that warms up and opens and closes automatically. The over-sized tub has sixteen Jacuzzi-jets and the roof panel slides open so, while soaking, couples can watch the moon over Diamond Head. She has stocked the bathroom with more Vera Wang home products, including candles, soaps, shampoo, lotions, and perfumes.

The suite is also meant for comfort and relaxation. The detail-oriented Wang designed and oversaw its completion down to even what movies the suite offers in the DVD player for its big-screen plasma TV. They include Wang's favorites, *The King and I* (a romantic musical), *When Harry Met Sally* (a romantic comedy), *Lost in Translation* (an Asian-themed dramatic comedy), and *Love Actually* (another romantic comedy.)

The hotel also offers a Vera Wang boutique downstairs accessible to all. Even those not staying at the resort can shop for her jewelry, home products, sunglasses, and resort clothing.

A model wears a design from Vera Wang's fall 2006 fashion collection.

She developed a line of hand creme, with special attention to the shape of the jar to be just to her tastes so the crème could be removed easily without spillage.

Wang even designed professional football cheerleader uniforms for the Philadelphia Eagles cheer squad. She modernized them by shedding the old-fashioned little skirts that traditionally ornament cheer costumes. She replaced them with sporty two-piece outfits with white form-fitting short-shorts and white jog-bra style tops ridged across the chest band with black border to provide contrast as well as support.

Perhaps Wang's most enduring accomplishment is how she fashioned herself into the expert on all things romantic. Brides turned to her for help getting through one of the most emotional times in their lives. Actor Billy Baldwin showed up at her salon recruiting Wang to help him propose to his girlfriend, singer Chynna Phillips. Baldwin borrowed one hundred wedding dresses and took them upstairs to a room in the Carlyle Hotel, where Wang's flagship boutique presides. Inside the dress-filled room he lit and set the table with champagne and caviar. He proposed by asking Phillips which of the gowns she wanted to wear on their wedding day.

Wang also got to see another of her creations as a guest at the wedding of the daughter of former Vice President Al Gore in 1997. "For the dress, we had a good idea: to keep it classical and minimal with a beautiful drape. I wanted it to have the dignity benefiting the daughter of the Vice President, but with a modern twist."

The service in Washington's National Cathedral was perfect, she said. "It was one of the most memorable times of my life."

One of Wang's most daring ventures has been the launch of a budget fashion line called Simply Vera at Kohl's department stores in 2007. The line offers clothes for the average woman who wants more style at affordable prices. Most items retail for under one hundred dollars. She joins other major designers such as Michael Graves and Isaac Mizrahi who took the challenge to create great design at budget prices with their items for Target discount stores.

As Wang says in support of her Simply Vera line, it's about clothes that make women look and feel better: "Personal style for me is about comfort," she said. "Casual can be extremely stylish. Dressy can be casual."

To balance her sometimes seventeen-hour work days, Wang spends weekends and holidays with her family at one of their weekend getaway houses and vacation homes. For a time they had a place in Pound Ridge, New York, where they stayed in a two hundred-year-old barn converted into a home. Her parents kept a home on their estate nearby. On Wang's ninety-four-acre estate outside of Manhattan she designed another weekend retreat. The house sits on a lake where they like to swim, fish and go boating in warm weather. In the winter, they go skating upon the frozen pond. The Wang-Becker family also has a vacation home in the exclusive beach resort community of Southampton, where such celebrities as Oprah Winfrey and Steven Spielberg also keep homes.

Vera Wang has lived an amazing life with no sign of letting go of the gold medal at the top of the fashion world. "I was a total fashion insider who became an outsider when I did bridal," Wang says. "I waited a long time to get to this stage. Women are real works of art, and I try to remember that that's what makes it worthwhile, that it's not just about making money . . . It's about pleasure, giving it to other people and getting it."

Vera Wang thanks the audience following her show in New York
in September 2005.

A model wears a design by Vera Wang during the presentation
of her spring 2008 bridal collection, in New York.

Timeline

1949:   Born on June 27 in New York City.

1957:   Receives first pair of ice skates for Christmas.

1959:   Wins first ice skating championship.

1968:   Fails to win place on U.S. Olympic team at National Figure Skating Championships; studies pre-medicine at Sarah Lawrence College.

1969:   Places fifth in Nationals with pairs partner; suffers breakdown and depression after skating partner leaves her.

1970:   Drops out of Sarah Lawrence; moves to Paris; works as a shopgirl at designer boutique Yves Saint Laurent; enrolls in the Sorbonne.

1971:   Returns home and graduates from Sarah Lawrence; decides on career in fashion design, but father refuses to pay for schooling; contacts editor at *Vogue* magazine and wins an entry-level job.

1986:   Takes job as design director for Ralph Lauren.

1989:   Marries Arthur Becker, designs her own bridal gown; quits job at Ralph Lauren.

1990:   Opens bridal salon in New York's Carlyle Hotel after father invests $4 million for her to start her own business.

1991:   Adopts first child, Cecelia.

1992:   Creates high-fashion Olympic ice skating dress for Nancy Kerrigan; launches line of evening gowns.

1993:   Adopts second child, Josephine.

1995:   Opens second salon, Maids on Madison, for wedding attendants.

1997:   Licenses a line of wedding shoes.

1999:   Branches into licensing for leathers and furs.

2000:   Signs deal to produce fragrance inspired by romantic feelings of wedding day.

2001:   Licenses china and dishes; publishes *Vera Wang on Weddings*.

2004:   Mother, Florence, dies.

2005:   Opens one-of-a-kind luxury resort hotel room in Hawaii, the Vera Wang Suite, suitable for honeymooners.

2006:   Father dies.

2007:   Launches Simply Vera line with Kohl's department store; buys her late parents' Park Avenue apartment for $23 million.

Sources

Chapter One | Inspiration

p. 11, "I fell in love . . ." Vera Wang, as told to Heather Won Tesoriero, "Turning Points: Ice Dreams," *Time*, February 18, 2002.

p. 12, "I had a mother . . ." "Aisles of Style," *Time*, September 21, 2007.

p. 12, "I had an immense . . ." Ibid.

p. 15, "They were both rebellious . . ." Alex Witchel, "From Aisle To Runway; Vera Wang," *New York Times*, June 19, 1994.

p 19, "What a fantasy land . . ." Shane Mitchell, "Vera Wang's Favorite Places," *Travel + Leisure*, October 2005.

Chapter Two | Vera Takes Off

p. 21, "she performed flawlessly . . ." "Vera Wang Takes Title in Skating," *New York Times*, March 12, 1960.

p. 21, "exceedingly graceful . . ." "Vera Wang Wins Skate Title Here," *NewYork Times*, March 11, 1967.

p. 22, "She was very . . ." Katherine Krohn, *Vera Wang: Enduring Style* (Minneapolis, Minn., Twenty-First Century Books, Lifeline Biographies 2009), 14.

p. 22, "At the end of a day . . ." Michelle Kwan, *Michelle Kwan: Heart of a Champion* (New York: Scholasatic Inc.,1997), 55.

p. 23, "I was always . . ." Vera Wang, http://verawang.me/quotes.

p. 25, "I always seemed . . ." Wang, "Turning Points: Ice Dreams," *Time*, February 18, 2002.

p 31, "When I didn't make . . ." Ibid.

Chapter Three | Pairing Up

p. 35-36, "During this time . . ." Wang, *Time*, February 18, 2002.

p. 36, "I had to learn . . ." "Aisles of Style," *Time*, September 21, 2007.

p. 36, "With the end . . ." Wang, *Time*, February 18, 2002.

p. 37, "He thought the chances . . ." Amy Larocca, "Vera Wang's Second Honeymoon," *New York* magazine, January 14, 2006.

p. 40, "I knew the world . . ." Barbara Krantrowitz, Holly Peterson, and Pat Wingert, "How I Got There," *Newsweek*, October 24, 2005.

p. 40-41, "I come from . . ." Alex Witchel, "From Aisle To Runway; Vera Wang," *New York Times*, June 19, 1994.

Chapter Four | Oh So *Vogue*

p 45, "*Vogue* is a seductive . . ." Krantrowitz, "How I Got There."

Chapter Six | Ripping Out the Seams of Tradition

p. 59, "Our kind of bridal salon . . . " Witchel, "From Aisle To Runway; Vera Wang."

p. 62-63, "We're prudent people . . ."Anne M. Todd, *Vera Wang: Asian Americans of Achievement* (New York: Chelsea House Publishers, and imprint of Infobase Publishing, 2007), 38.

p. 63, "For most women . . ." Vera Wang, *Vera Wang On Weddings*, (New York: HarperCollins, 2001), 136.

p. 66, "the dress should . . ." Ibid.

p. 67, "If I were to listen to . . ." Witchel, "From Aisle To Runway; Vera Wang."

Chapter Seven | Olympic Dreams: The Triumphant Sequel

p. 70, "You can't believe the technology . . ." Jill Gerston, "Spinning Dreams," *New York Times*, February 13, 1994.

p: 72, " When you're skating . . ." Nancy Kerrigan, *Artistry on Ice: Figure Skating Skills and Style* (Champagne, Ill: Human Kinetics, 2003), 214.

p. 74, "It's one of my favorite . . ." Gerston, "Spinning Dreams."

p. 74, "Why? . . ." Martha Duffy, *Time*, January 17, 1994.

Chapter Eight | Brand Vera

p.86, "The magic is in weightless . . ." Katherine Krohn, *Vera Wang: Enduring Style* (Minneapolis, Minn.: Twenty-First Century Books, Lifeline Biographies 2009), 52.

p. 90, "As in fashion . . ." Elif Sungur, *Dexigner.com*, November 18, 2005 www.dexigner.com/design_news/3606.html.

p. 94, "For the dress . . ." Ibid, 56.

p. 94, "It was one of . . ." Ibid.

p. 95, "Personal style for me is . . ." Vera Wang, YouTube on Simply Vera, October 2, 2007, www.youtube.come/watch?v=4uRvPCzeutl.

p. 95, "I was a total fashion insider . . ." Larocca, "Vera Wang's Second Honeymoon."

p. 95, "I waited a long time . . ." Witchel, "From Aisle To Runway; Vera Wang."

Bibliography

Selected Books

Critchell, Samantha. "Vera Wang takes pride in artistry on ice." *Boston Globe*, January 13, 2010.

Gerston, Jill. "Spinning Dreams." *New York Times*, February 13, 1994.

Halpern, Adena. *Target Underwear and a Vera Wang Gown*. New York: Gotham Books, Penguin Group, 2006.

Kantrowitz, Barbara, Holly Peterson, and Pat Wingert. "How I Got There: Eight prominent women give first-person accounts of turning points in their personal lives and careers. What these leaders all display is a continuing passion for their work." *Newsweek*, October 24, 2005.

Kerrigan, Nancy. *Artistry on Ice: Figure Skating Skills and Style*. Champagne, Ill: Human Kinetics, 2003.

Krohn, Katherine. *Vera Wang: Enduring Style*. Minneapolis, Minn.: Twenty-First Century Books (Lifeline Biographies), 2009.

Kwan, Michelle. *Michelle Kwan: Heart of a Champion*. New York: Scholastic Inc., 1997.

Larocca, Amy. "Vera Wang's Second Honeymoon." *New York* magazine, January 14, 2006.

Louie, Elaine. "Two Skaters Give Couture a Whirl." *New York Times*, February 16, 1992.

Mitchell, Shane. "Vera Wang's Favorite Places." *Travel and Leisure*, October 2005.

Nemy, Enid. "64 Presented at International Debutante Ball." *New York Times*, December 31, 1968.

Rogers, Thomas. "Victorious Contestant Gets Spectator's Eye View of Skating Tourney: Miss Wang Takes Senior Class in No. Atlantic Figure Skating: Delights the Audience." *New York Times*, December 17, 1967.

Rogers, Thomas. "Figure Skaters Olympics-Bound: Wood, Miss Fleming Head Strongly Rated U.S. Team." *New York Times*, January 23, 1968.

Song, Jaymes. "$4,000-a-night Vera Wang Suite officially opens." *USA Today*, June 1, 2005.

Spindler, Amy M. "Patterns: Engineered athletic wear." *New York Times*. May 10, 1994.

Sungur, Elif. "Icons Halekulani & Vera Wang Define A New Standard of Guest Experience." Dexigner.com, November 18, 2005.

Todd, Anne M. *Vera Wang: Asian Americans of Achievement*. New York: Chelsea House Publishers, 2007.

Wang, Vera. "Ice Dreams: The noted fashion designer tells what she gained from failing to be an Olympic skater." *Time*, February 18, 2002.

Wang, Vera. *Vera Wang on Weddings*. New York: William Morrow, 2001.

Werden, Lincoln A. "Vera Wang, 12-year-old Skater, Captures Junior Laurels Here; Daughter of Chinese Parents Scores as Middle Atlantic Championships Open." *New York Times*, March 3, 1962.

Wilson, Eric. "Vera Wang's Business Is no Longer All Dressed in White." *New York Times*, December 15, 2005.

Witchel, Alex. "From Aisle to Runway; Vera Wang." *New York Times*, June 19, 1994.

"Vera Wang Wed To Arthur Becker." *New York Times*, June 23, 1989.

"Miss Fleming, 18, Keeps Skate Title: Takes U.S. Senior Women's Event 4th Year in Row." *New York Times*. January 22, 1967.

Paid Notice: Deaths, Wang, C.C., *New York Times*, October 1, 2006.

Paid Notice: Deaths WANG, FLORENCE WU, *New York Times*, January 27, 2004.

Web Sites

www.verawangonweddings.com.
Designer's Web site complete with both bridal and other fashions and designs. Includes videos including excerpts from her book and other guidance on all things bridal.

http://www.halekulani.com/accommodations/vera_wang_suite/
Official site for the Hotel Halekulani that houses the Vera Wang Suite. Includes details on suite's design and features and photos of the suite.

http://nymag.com/fashion/fashionshows/designers/bios/verawang/
A guide to the latest from the designer, plus biographical information and design milestones.

http://www.worldskatingmuseum.org/
The Hall of Fame of figure skating includes names and brief biographical imformation on major forces on the art of skating including Vera Wang.

http://www.usfsa.org/
Official site of the United States Figure Skating team. Includes videos of great skating performances including champions wearing Vera Wang creations.

Glossary

Charmeuse: Lightweight delicate fabric with a satin weave, front has a shiny finish. Can be made of silk or synthetics. The luster and delicacy make it suited to lingerie, flowing evening gowns and bridal gowns.

Competition dress: For special events and contests, figure skaters wear flashier special outfits designed to catch the judges' eyes to hopefully draw bigger scores. Skaters sometimes resort to outlandish dresses to try and stand out on televised events.

Duchesse satin: a Vera Wang staple in high-end gowns, because of its elegant and lustrous shine. Its softer texture is created from many layers of delicate fiber. She believes satin looks "important."

Fashion Week: New designs are unveiled by major designers generally twice a year in fashion centers like New York and Paris. Collections are shown in fashion shows over a period of days. Collections for autumn/ winter are shown usually around February, and spring/summer collections are shown around September. Ready-to-wear fashion weeks occur separately and earlier than those of haute couture.

Freeskate: For figure skaters competing in singles, or solo skating, they can perform to music of their choosing and perform whatever moves they please, within the time limit required (4 minutes for female skaters, 4 ½ minutes for male skaters).

Haute couture or couture: French phrase from the longtime center of fashion meaning literally "high sewing" or "high dressmaking." Exclusive custom-fitted clothing generally higher quality materials sewn with more attention to detail, thereby costing more in time, materials and expertise.

Illusion: A very fine delicate netting used for veils and see-through inserts into clothing, can come in any color.

Licensing: Legal agreement to produce goods under one name by another company.

Ready-to-Wear: Factory-made clothing sold in standardized sizes that fit most people off the rack and meant to be worn without significant alteration. Uses standard patterns and factories for faster construction to keep costs lower.

Red Carpet: Traditionally used to mark the route taken by important people, from royalty to politicians to celebrities at formal events.
Satin: Woven fabric with glossy surface, common in wedding gowns

Sheath: A type of dress fitting tightly to the body. Often made of a very light and thin material like r silk, and rarely contains any flourishes. Typical length falls around the knees or lower thighs.

Silk taffeta, silk radzmere, and taffeta blends: light and airy fabric that comes in different weights and textures but is light and airy, and rustles.

Spandex: a super-stretchy synthetic fabric that is durable and holds its shape. Common in skating outfits to allow full movement

Tulle: lightweight very fine netting, that can be made of either silk, nylon, or rayon. Common in bridal veils, gowns and ballet tutus. Used to be used in petticoats as undergarments but Wang likes it on its own on the outside because it offers a look of femininity.

Index

Picture Credits

2-3:	AP Photo/Dima Gavrysh
8:	AP Photo/Louis Lanzano
10:	Beverly Brown / Alamy
12-13:	Peter Barritt / Alamy
16-17:	Used under license from iStockphoto.com
19:	Used under license from iStockphoto.com
20-21:	Used under license from iStockphoto.com
23:	AP Photo/Lionel Cironneau
24:	AP Photo/Amy Sancetta, File
26-27:	AP Photo/Mary Altaffer
28-29:	AP Photo
32:	PCN Photography / Alamy
34-35:	AP Photo
37:	Used under license from iStockphoto.com
38-39:	PCL / Alamy
42-43:	Alex Hibbert / Alamy
44-45:	Antiques & Collectables / Alamy
46:	Ambient Images Inc. / Alamy
48:	Used under license from iStockphoto.com
50:	Sandra Baker / Alamy
52-53:	ALY SONG/Reuters /Landov
55:	AP Photo/Seth Wenig
56-57:	AP Photo/Louis Lanzano
58:	Patrick Batchelder / Alamy
60-61:	AP Photo/Louis Lanzano
64-65:	AP Photo/Louis Lanzano
68:	AP Photo/Denis Paquin
70-71:	AP Photo/Sal Veder
73:	AP Photo/Charles Krupa, File
75:	AP Photo/Doug Mills
77:	AP Photo/Doug Mills
78:	AP Photo/Doug Mills, File
80:	AP Photo/Mary Altaffer
82:	AP Photo/Bebeto Matthews
84-85:	AP Photo/Greg Gibson
86-87:	AP Photo/Dima Gavrysh
88-89:	AP Photo/Mary Altaffer
92-93:	AP Photo/Bebeto Matthews
96-97:	AP Photo/John Smock
98:	AP Photo/Richard Drew